To: _____

From: _____

HOW
TO
LIVE

Published by Sellers Publishing, Inc.
161 John Roberts Road, South Portland, ME 04106
Visit us at www.sellerspublishing.com • E-mail: rsp@rsvp.com

© 2016 Sellers Publishing, Inc.
Text and illustrations copyright © 2016 Sandy Gingras

All rights reserved.

ISBN-13: 978-1-4162-4580-3

No portion of this book may be reproduced or transmitted in any form,
or by any means, electronic or mechanical, including photographing,
recording, or by any information and storage retrieval system, without
written permission from the publisher.

Printed and bound in China.

10 9 8 7 6 5 4 3 2 1

HOW TO LIVE

by Sandy Gingras

SELLERS
PUBLISHING

When my son was in kindergarten, his school had "Back to School Night." All of the parents sat at tiny desks while the kids stood in front of the blackboard. One by one, the kids stepped forward and said what they wanted to be when they grew up as a picture they had drawn of themselves in that role projected onto a screen.

Johnny wanted to be a fireman (picture of a guy in a red truck). Jane wanted to be an astronaut (rocket ship going up). When it got to my son's turn, he stepped forward as a giant blue blob appeared on the screen. ALL the parents leaned forward and squinted. WHAT THE HECK WAS THAT?

Then my son said, in his determined little voice, "When I grow up, I want to be a whale."

I wanted to cry with happiness. My son was a dreamer. A BIG dreamer.

He's graduating from college now and on the brink of a new life. I wrote this book as a kind of graduation present to him. But, as I was writing it, I realized that I was writing it for myself too (and all of us who are trying to renew ourselves and make

our lives better). Because I think
we're all students--and every
day we're graduating from now into
tomorrow. And I believe that
every day we need reminders of
how to live...

← room in head
for more
wisdom

← room in heart
to grow...

...and nudges to keep on

dreaming big.

Remember that no one else has ever gone down your path. It is uniquely yours.

So you'll have to make your own way.

Every step, you can choose fear

or you can choose Life.

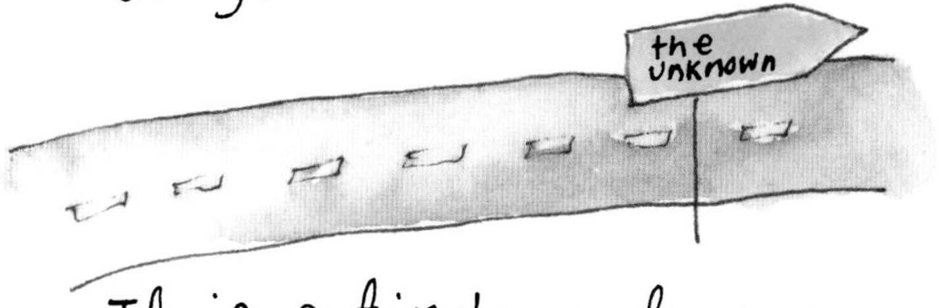

It is entirely up to you.

Sometimes, you may feel alone and confused.
I can't make sense of the directions. Part B goes where?
insert
LiFe
Z
A
X
P
C
H
B

But, if you follow your heart, you'll find that a heart is its own kind of map.

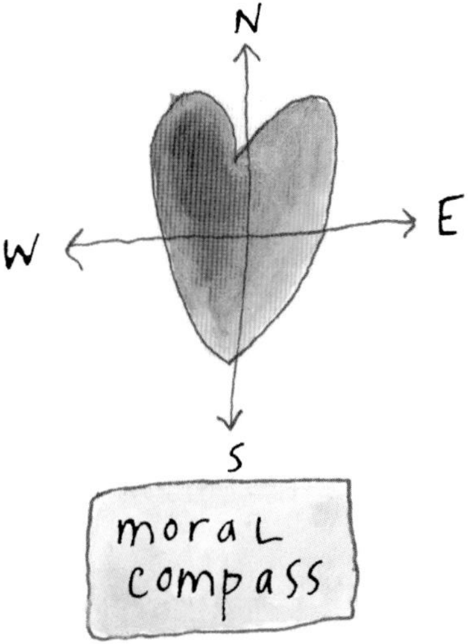

N

W ← → E

S

moral compass

And if you go where your heart takes you,

you'll never go wrong.

So, go gently into the world.

Wonder and be awed--
because every moment
is a miracle.

Be kind to others,

especially those
less fortunate.

Because we are all connected.

Don't ever be so set upon
your own journey

that you don't stop to let
the duck family cross
the road.

Be a force of goodness.

That is the greatest
strength of all.

Always keep your beautiful imagination.

So sharpen your pencil

and do the best that you can.

Remember that impossible things become possible if you want them enough.

And
the best way
to get something

done is just to
begin.

WORK

honestly,

humbly

and

hard.

Grow a little every day.

Worry Less.

tangled
up
and
paralyzed
by
anxiety

(mistakes are just
choices that you make,
and each one has its
own lessons and
rewards).

Balance.

Go outside

and play.

Do one thing

at

a

time.

Every day is a
new beginning, so

rise
and

shine!

READ!

Love true

and Loyal.

Sing in the shower.

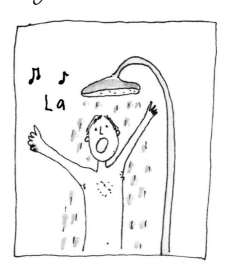

Call home.

Belly Laugh

Believe and be
positive!

You are always
stronger than you
think you are.

And

GROWTH HAS
NO LIMITS

Don't underestimate slow and steady.

Remember that even huge elephants go vast distances one step at a time.

Give yourself a
permission slip
to say YES!
to Life...

magical...creative...free...in the moment...spontaneous...

Some days you'll
have to create
your own
sunshine.

Always
remember
that

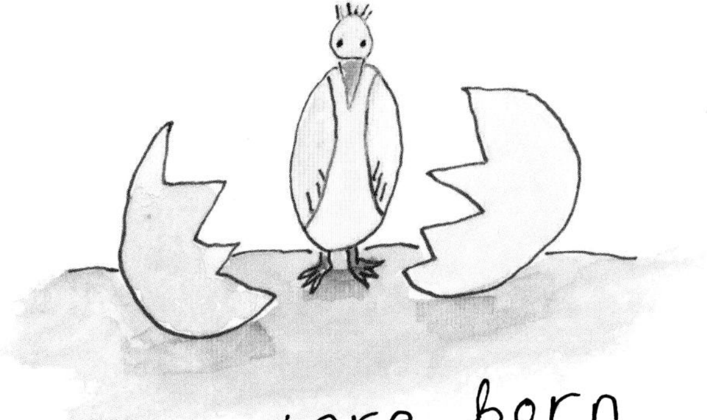

you were born
to fly.

Trust.

Even when it storms,
because there will be
better weather ahead.

Have faith that this, too, shall pass...

Life is full of gifts

arriving unexpectedly.

So look around you
every day and be
grateful for what you have.

MY LIST OF
WHAT I'M THANKFUL
FOR

1. _____
2. _____
3. _____
4. _____
5. _____
6. _____ turn page
for more →

Do this, especially when times are hard, and thankfulness will be

a light to guide you through even the darkest places

Never forget
that you are
Loved deeply
for who
you
are...

"Live your life!
Live your Life!
Live your Life!"

—Maurice Sendak